Etude

Jean Sibelius, Op. 76. Nr. 2.

Leggiero

p
segue
Ped.
p
Ped.
p

mp
f
p
poco rit.
mf
Ped.
Ped.

13 MORCEAUX

POUR LE PIANO

Op. 76 No. 1. Esquisse
— - 2. Etude
— - 3. Carillon
— - 4. Humoresque
— - 5. Consolation
— - 6. Romanzetta
— - 7. Affettuoso
— - 8. Pièce enfantine
— - 9. Arabesque
— - 10. Elegiaco
— - 11. Linnaea
— - 12. Capriccietto
— - 13. Harlequinade

Jean Sibelius

Op. 76

EDITION WILHELM HANSEN

17710

PRINTED IN DENMARK BY WIL-TRYK, RINGSTED